Introduction
Thank You for Coming

Hi there and thanks for stopping by. My name's Matt and like you school didn't teach me about how to handle my money and finances. My parents weren't that much help either, they came from the old school mentality of "you have to figure it out yourself" which is fine and dandy sometimes but for most people it just doesn't work. You need to put your head down and hit the grindstone in whatever you want to do in life. There are no shortcuts or easy buttons, but with some proper direction and guidance in the beginning you will come out fine in the end. We all define success and wealth differently. Find your definitions and what it truly means to you. Don't ever compromise yourself and use this workbook as a jumping off point to get started. There's a ton about wealth creation and money management that they don't teach you in schools for a variety of reasons, this is a workbook to help you get some initial direction. Some ideas are simple and easy to get started and some are a bit out there, don't worry, take that first step and just work on moving forward. My hope is that this workbook will inspire you towards a lifelong passion of self-development and learning.

To All Your Future Successes,

Matt Malouf

Quotes

"Yesterday is only a dream, tomorrow is only a vision. But today will live. Make every yesterday a dream of happiness, and every tomorrow a vision of hope. Look well, therefore, to this day." – Kālidāsa

"It is far better to be associated with a few who are right than with the mob which is wrong, because right is always the winner in the end." – Niccolò Machiavelli

"We should make a personal goal of becoming a "transition person," a person who changes the scripts transferred to the next generation from negative to positive by being proactive. This should be part of our personal mission statement. A tendency that has run through a family for generations can stop with one person." – Anwar Sadat, the former President of Egypt

Secret #1: Increase Your Teachability Index

- You have to be coachable (teachable)
    - Being coachable is about opening your mind up and listening to new ideas and methods of doing things

- You must be teachable
    - Be an excellent student and be willing to learn
    - How teachable are you?

<u>On a scale of 1 to 10 [with 10 being most open]</u>

What is your willingness to learn this information?
1   2   3   4   5   6   7   8   9   10

What is your willingness to accept change?
1   2   3   4   5   6   7   8   9   10

"If you want things in your life to change, then you have to change things in your life"

Your next 5 years will be like the last 5 if you don't change something.

Secret #2: The Training – Balance Scale

The Training Balance Scale is the HOW and the WHY, and that there must always be balance between the two.

- Side A– motivation, thinking, thoughts, dreams, your WHY.

- Side B– actions! What are you good at? Skills, techniques, physical action. The HOW.

The thought process is more important the how

Side A	Side B
What drives you?	What are you good at?
Motivation	Actions
Thoughts	Skills
Dreams	Techniques
Your Why	Physical Action

The proper mentality and thought process is more important than the how
However, there must be a balance between the two sides

Secret #3: Understand the 4 Phases

The following four phases are the process we move through towards achieving our dreams whether it is in school, sports or business.

Phase 1: Unconscious Incompetence
You don't know what you don't know

Phase 2: Conscious Incompetence
You know there's something you don't know

Phase 3: Conscious Competence
Thinking through the process, make conscious effort to apply new knowledge

Phase 4: *Unconscious* Competence
Habit and automatic

Secret #4: Set That Goal

Webster's Dictionary defines a goal as the end result toward which effort is directed.

So, to what and how do we direct our efforts?

- Have a specific goal and a clearly defined dream.

- Clearly defined goals will give you a target to your forward progress.

- Focus is the key to start off with, diversification comes later.

- To find that one thing you can focus on and become an expert.

<u>I will score more goals this season is NOT a goal!</u>

<u>In our 23 games I will score 15 goals while playing forward.</u> This is better. You can measure the outcome of this.

Proper goals are **<u>narrow</u>** in scope, have a **<u>definitive</u>** purpose, **<u>clearly defined</u>** dream and a burning **<u>desire</u>** to achieve it.

If you truly know yourself, you know what you are good at and what you enjoy doing then you will have the proper guidance to wealth and happiness.

Become known for something! What is it you want to be known for?

Secret #5: The Law of Attraction

The Law of Attraction Simply states:

"You will bring to yourself what you ask for."

Utilize the Law of Attraction- whatever you focus on and think about in your mind you will attract it to your life. Whatever you really want (or don't want) you will bring to your life.

Good thoughts/feelings vs. Bad thoughts/feelings If you are always negative about your life and situation then more negativity will seemingly come your direction. We cannot control what happens only how we react to what has happened to us.

Watch the movie "The Secret"

- The Law of Attraction is the law of nature. It is as impartial as the law of gravity.
- Nothing can come into your experience unless you summon it through persistent thoughts.
- Your thoughts determine your frequency and your feelings tell you immediately what frequency you are on. When you feel bad you are on the frequency of drawing more bad things. When you feel good, you are powerfully attracting more good things to you.

Secret #6: Read, Read and Read

* Must read books *

Leaders are always readers- read books, books change people. The books you read today will determine the person you will be in 5 years.

What's in your personal library? What should be in your personal library?

Examples: The Law of Success in 16 Lessons, Ask and it is Given, The Magic of Thinking Big, Over the Top, The Magic of Believing, The Go Getter, How to Win Friends and Influence People, Rich Dad Poor Dad, Think and Grow Rich.

Read books everyday.

Reread the great books over and over again, you will gain something new each time based on new experiences.

Secret #7: Listen to Recordings

Listen to CDs and podcasts: Listen to information in audio format about success, motivation and attitude. Constantly feed your mind with positive information everyday. We are bombarded with negative influences everyday. Replace these negative influences with positive and productive thoughts to create new patterns and ideas.

Work on your thinking to help with your Training Balance Scale.

Ex. Podcasts are a great inexpensive way to get your daily refreshers.

Example: think of the great athletes and actors who work on and hone their craft everyday.

 *Train yourself positively everyday.*

Secret #8: Attend Seminars

Improve by education.

Regularly attending seminars gets you in a room with like-minded people and having an experiential event. Continuing your education in a format with like-minded people, your thoughts will be more inline with others in success.

More than the knowledge, techniques, motivation, dream building, tips and advice you get at the seminar; it's the experience you have that changes you. Constantly continuing education with like minded people so they are thinking right, their thoughts are aligned and moving closer to Unconscious Competence.

Secret #9: Keep 10% for Yourself

Pay Yourself First!!

You earned it! So you deserve to keep some of it. From whatever you earn peel off at least 10% right away for yourself, for *your* future.

SAVE 10%

The Richest Man in the World once said that *all successful people save*. Live within your means–it's a lie, to achieve real wealth you must live below your means.

Secret #10: Good Debt Management

Get out of bad debt! Reduce your debt load, interest load, fees, and payments. Know the difference of crippling debt and the use of credit.

Like a hammer debt can be used to build up or take down, it depends on how it is used. The wealthiest people use debt properly to increase their net worth and make it work for them.

Good Debt is debt that is used to buy appreciating assets that will put more money into my pocket = mortgages, business loans, etc.

Bad Debt is debt that is used to buy depreciating assets that lose money over time and do not put money into my pocket = car loans, personal credit cards carrying a balance Crippling Debt vs. Use of Credit

So what is Debt?

Simply put, debt is a financial obligation (or burden) to someone else.

Secret #11: Manage Priorities

Good priority management- you can't manage time! Prioritize your to do's. Reduces stress confusion and anxiety, get things done in less time and with better focus.

Make a daily list of items you need to do that day, and then from that list prioritize them by order of importance.

Example:

Your Daily/ Weekly/ Monthly Items List		
Things To Do	People to Call	Appointments

Secret #12: Associate with Winners

Associate with winners- associate with like-minded people, income will be the average of their five best friends. If you continue to do as you've always done you'll get what you've always got. Associate with and be in the presence of rich people.

"Tell me who your friends are and I will tell you who you are."
What do you think this quote means?

Find where rich people hang out and go there.

_____, _____, _____,

The 5 Association Activity

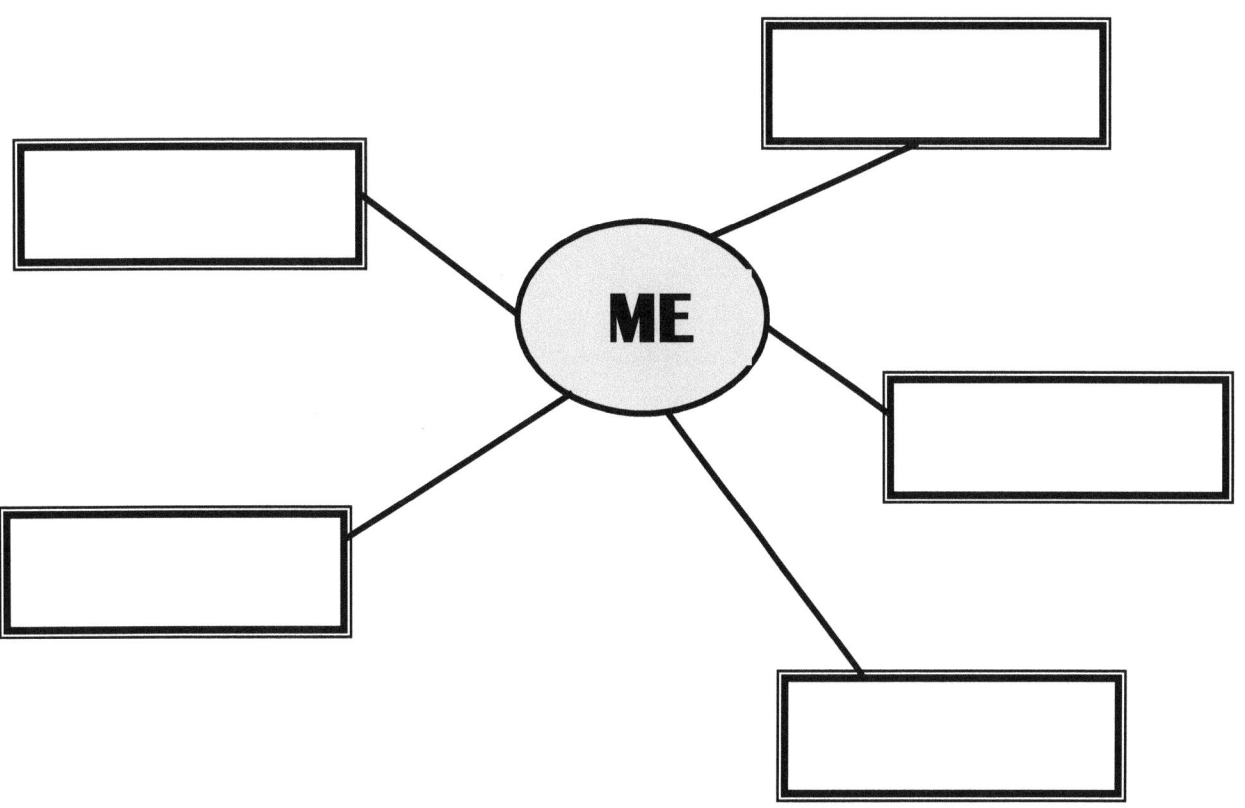

The thought process, attitudes and energy of your closest associations will rub off on you.

Secret #13: Work

It's called work for a reason, because it's not easy and many times not even fun. However, that comes back to doing what you **love**!

Work Hard vs. Work Smart

Work- misunderstood principle, what is work? Work hard or smart? The work is the thought process and not the physical doing.

Do what you love, then it's not work; put 12 hours into something but it's not work, be blissfully happy doing the activity. You don't do work, you understand work. Do activities and put in the time and create results.

Have you ever failed at anything? No

Secret #14: Develop a Pleasing Personality

Develop a pleasing personality- be likable.

How to Win Friends and Influence People by Dale Carnegie

Be friendly and nice to others, the golden rule.

Secret #15: Develop Communication Skills

Develop communication skills- learn to be persuasive and be able to negotiate well, sell your ideas to another person, put a deal together. Focus on becoming better.

The most important part (and the hardest) is to develop your ear and be a great listener. What is the other person telling you? Or not telling you?

Only 10% of all communication is the words we use.

Great communication skill is the ability to express yourself clearly and at the same time have the ability to truly listen.

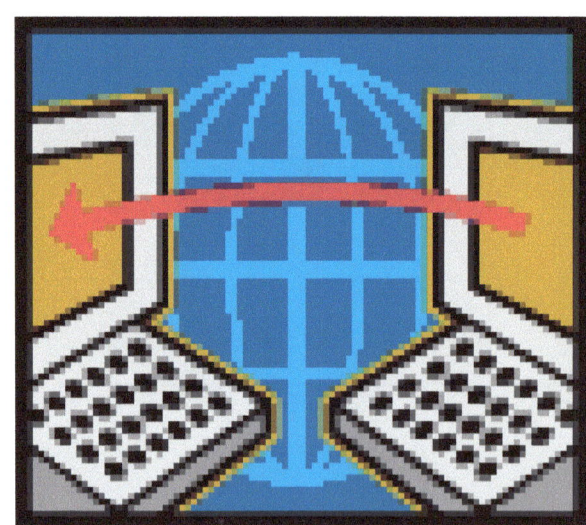

Secret #16: Improve Your Good Name

1. Your credit score is your financial report card that nobody ever told you how to pass or get good grades on. Many things that you think are right are plain wrong and won't help you.

2. Continuously strive to improve your credit score- so that you can use Other People's Money (OPM).

If you have a great credit score then you will pay less interest fees and have the opportunity to use more credit to build your wealth. This will also allow you to gain even more leverage to use other people's money, to acquire more assets to create your wealth.

Secret #17: Reduce and Optimize Expenses

The easiest way to reduce expenses is through tax savings and insurance premium savings and to reduce debt.

Reduce taxes- there are over 15,000 rules and regulations and over 200,000 pages of tax code. The wealthiest people pay little to no taxes and the little guy pays the most. Reduce taxes to increase cash flow.

Why is this? A good knowledge of the tax code and a knowledgeable CPA are vital.

Reduce the amount of insurance premiums you pay (life, health, auto, etc) reduce by ½ at least. You still need to make sure that you have the proper coverage for your particular situation.

Secret #18: Use Corporations and Trusts

Use corporations and trusts for tax efficiency, asset protection and increasing ability to get lines of credit. Starting corporations, how to use them, how to legally reduce taxes and get extended lines of credit.

It is easier to get more credit through corporations than for your personal self.

This one takes A LOT of work and there is little info out there so be forewarned you will spend a lot of time educating yourself should you choose to do this.

Secret #19: OPM (Other People's Money)

Learn to use OPM (Other People's Money).

Success Through a Positive Mental Attitude- by W. Clement Stone.

You have to utilize OPM to be successful. You can't do it all on your own so you will have to use other people's money to grow your own net worth.

Secret #20: Increase Your Income

You have to get your thinking right to get to thoughts to create abundance, reduce expenses and increase income.

Focus on increasing income:
1. Investing in real estate with no money down, real estate business etc
2. EBay and Facebook Marketplace allow you to get started without any cash or money and don't even have to leave the house to work on it.
3. Investing in the markets (very challenging) through stocks, bonds, or commodities.
4. Trading in stocks very different from investing where you buy and sell at a rapid pace.
5. Through some type of network marketing opportunity (very difficult, competition)

Building a character of total integrity and living a life of love and service that creates such unity isn't easy, but it's plausible. If we start with the daily private victory and work from the inside out, results will surely come.

Well there you have it, congratulations! You've taken some positive steps towards your life dreams and goals. You were made to thrive and should live your life accordingly. Take some of what you've started on here, build on it, make it your own. Take ownership and responsibility for your finances and you will discover true wealth.

I wish you all the success in the world.

www.ingramcontent.com/pod-product-compliance
Lightning Source LLC
Chambersburg PA
CBHW051838210526
45473CB00005B/1935